EXPOSING THE SCOFFERS

SIGNS OF THE ENDTIME!

Dr. Joe Van Koevering

Unless otherwise indicated, all scripture quotations are taken from the King James Version of the Bible.

EXPOSING THE SCOFFERS SIGNS OF THE ENDTIME!

Copyright©2001

Dr. Joe VanKoevering
God's News Behind the News
P.O. Box 10475
St. Petersburg, FL 33733

ISBN Number: 0-939241-87-0

Printed in the United States of America

EXPOSING THE SCOFFERS
SIGNS OF THE ENDTIME!

"Knowing this first, that there shall come in the **last days scoffers**, *walking after their own lusts, [4]And saying, Where is the promise of his coming? for since the fathers fell asleep, all things continue as they were from the beginning of the creation. [5]For this they willingly are ignorant of, that by the word of God the heavens were of old, and the earth standing out of the water and in the water: [6]Whereby the world that then was, being overflowed with water, perished: [7]But the heavens and the earth, which are now, by the same word are kept in store, reserved unto fire against the day of judgment and perdition of ungodly men.*

[8]But, beloved, be not ignorant of this one thing, that one day is with the Lord as a thousand years, and a thousand years as one day.

[9]The Lord is not slack concerning his promise, as some men count slackness; but is longsuffering to us-ward, not willing that any should perish, but that all should come to repentance."

--2 Peter 3:3-9

I believe this is THE hour for the Church! The Last Days prophesied in the scriptures are upon us this very hour. Why? Because the SCOFFERS are emerging on all fronts; and namely within the Christian community itself!

As we have moved into the new millennium, the *"Christian scoffers"* are voicing their message, loud and strong. Today, these scoffers critically call us "doomsayers", who supposedly use "fear" and "madness" for the purpose of "cashing in" on naïve Believers.

But you will know the difference and discern between truth and lies.

These scoffers attempt to ridicule us for preaching that we are in the *"Last Days"*. Yet, little do they realize, that their very actions prove the New Testament writers, and support our claim that we ARE facing the very last days. The scoffers THEMSELVES are literal proof that we are in the last days.

If you listen carefully to much of the Church world today, you, too, can hear them asking, *"Oh, we've heard that before. Why not show me this promise that He is coming that you are always talking about?"* I guarantee you, the skeptics and critics of the soon return of Christ, are growing today!

Some well-known preachers today are telling people to no longer teach or believe in Bible prophecy. Some even recommend that you should not attend prophecy conferences. The purpose of this book is to prove with unequivocal documentation that they preach these lies today because they have a hidden agenda. If you do not have "ears to hear," many in the church are being duped into believing these lies.

Dear Friend and lover of Bible prophecy, brace yourself. We are next on the *"hit list"* to receive the abuse, scorn and ridicule of the *"witch hunters"* within the Body of Christ! These scoffers are themselves PROOF that we ARE correct when we say Jesus is coming very soon.

I want to present the group of scoffers that I believe present the greatest threat to the Body of Christ today. These scoffers are attempting to confuse you and rob you of your *"Blessed Hope"*.

Who are they? They are the PRETERISTS!

What is the *"Preterist view"* and why should we be concerned?

To most Christians, they have never even heard of the word "preterist". Yet, this growing number of vocal "scholars" are gaining new momentum within the church world, and must now be addressed.

The word *"preterist"* is simply a fancy word for *"past"* or *"past fulfillment"*. I am what is called a *"futurist"*. Simply put, the word "futurist" signifies that the Biblical "*Last Days*" are yet *"future"*. Yes, the tribulation is yet to come. The coming of Christ, rapture of the church, rise of the antichrist—these are all **FUTURE EVENTS**!

As *"futurists"*, we await and anticipate the rapture and return of Christ. The Book of Revelation is yet to be completely fulfilled. However, there are people, ministers, scholars, and theologians, who do **NOT** believe this! They are called "*preterists*". They believe that most, if not all of *"Bible prophecy"* has **ALREADY BEEN FULFILLED**! And, believe it or not, their ranks are growing!

"Now, Joe, let me get this straight. Are you telling me that there are Bible-believing ministers and Bible-believing theologians who actually believe that all Bible prophecy has already happened sometime?"

Yes!

"Joe, wait a minute. Are you telling me that there are Bible-believing people who say Jesus has already come back?"

Yes!

"Are you saying that there are people who preach that the anti-Christ already came; and everything Jesus said in Matthew 24 and everything John wrote in the Book of Revelation, has already happened?"

Yes!

"Well that would mean, Joe, that we must be in the millennium right now!"

I've got one thing to say to my Preterist brethren, and they are brethren. I'm not attacking individuals. I'm merely presenting truth.

If we're in the millennium now and this is the

Kingdom of God, I'm sorry I signed up for this deal. It better be getting a whole lot better than it is right now!

Through the next pages and footnotes, I am going to show you---in their own words---how ridiculous and absolutely false their statements are.

Please allow the Holy Spirit to give you discernment in your own heart.

In John Noe's book, "**BEYOND THE END TIMES**," he boldly states:

"As long as the others fail to recognize that 'the end' the Bible proclaims is behind us and not ahead of us, is past and not future, the answer is a resounding, YES! No consideration of the end times is complete without a look at the 'past fulfillment' of prophecy."[1]

He goes on to list a few things on the back cover of this book and he says, *"In this book you'll discover things like how the end for the world came right on time. How the time and nature of Christ's past return occurred... the true identity of the new Heaven and the new Earth and why the future is bright and promising"*[2]

There are other bold declarations inside this book.

"Sometime shortly after the turn of the millennium, I predict a paradigm shift away from the tyranny of termination and into the hopeful, scriptural truth of a world without end."[3]

*"Today we stand poised on the doorstep of the new millennium, and on the threshold of a new awakening. We moderns have not reached the point where reform is no longer needed. And biblical, end time prophecy is the next area ripe for reform."*4

Are you beginning to see now why we must begin to address this heretical teaching?

Preterist author Arther Melanson takes a "stab" at well known Bible prophecy author Hal Lindsey, and predicts: *"There is coming a time when a future generation will be saying, 'They used to believe what? And Hal Lindsey's books will be in a museum.'"*5

"**Last Day's Madness**," written by Gary DeMar, says, *"Last day's madness would be eliminated if Christians could be convinced, through a thorough study of Scripture, that the Olivet Discourse is a prophecy that was fulfilled by A.D. 70."*6

He goes on to say, *"The expression 'end of the age' refers 'to the end of the "Jewish age," i.e., the time of transference from a national (Israel only) to an international people of God, (the world),' What the Apostle Paul describes as the 'end of the ages,' a period of time that had come upon the First Century Church."*7

Are you beginning to understand their false message?

From a pamphlet entitled "**What is the Preterist**

<u>View?</u>"

"Scores of preterist books, tracts, video and audio tapes have been produced and many more are on the way. It's beginning to capture significant public attention and is 'spreading like wildfire' at the grass roots level."

"The final events of the redemptive drama came to pass in the first century within the apostles' generation(before A.D. 70). Christ's kingdom is here now. Paradise has been restored in Christ (spiritually speaking). We live in the Garden of Eden now (if we are in Christ)..."[8]

John MacArthur in his book entitled "**The Second Coming**," makes this observation,

"The position (speaking of this Preterist position) sounds so bizarre that some may wonder if it seriously deserves to be refuted. How could anyone claim to believe the Bible while denying that Christ will return bodily to earth? But the position has garnered an outspoken and increasing following, especially among young believers with more zeal than knowledge. Judging from views on the Internet and in other forums, it appears they are having phenomenal success proselytizing other undiscerning souls to their view."[9]

I agree wholeheartedly with that candid observation by John MacArthur. This is the reason why I felt so compelled, literally arrested by the Spirit of God, to address this issue with accuracy; by documenting their very own words, and let you discern the truth from the error.

Permit me to quote from more of their statements. I'm laying a foundation so you clearly understand what these men are teaching.

John Noe continues to write, *"The biblical last days are behind us, not ahead of us. They are in the past, not in the future. Every New Testament reference to the last days or equivalent 'last times, last hour', refers to the time its writers were living in the first century. They weren't the last days of planet Earth, or the end of time. They were the last days of the Old Covenant Jewish system and age. There are no exceptions."*[10]

Do you understand what he's saying?

Mr. DeMar attempts to defend his view in the following manner: *"But how can we maintain that Jesus 'came' in A.D. 70? Jesus 'coming' in judgment upon Jerusalem and His coming 'up to the Ancient of Days' (Daniel 7:13; Matthew 24:30) were two events that occurred within the time span of the first generation of Christians. There is no future fulfillment of these events."*[11]

David Chilton was one of the leading scholars of this movement. He was their leading theologian up until his death. In his book, "**Paradise Restored**," he summarizes the forty-five major arguments in his book. I'm only going to list a few of these. I'm not trying to shock you. I am trying to paint a picture for you with authenticity, verification and facts. Here are just a few of the forty-five major arguments that he makes in this book.

8. *"The wicked are 'raptured' first (i.e., driven out of the earth and disinherited), as the righteous increasingly come into possession of all things."*

11. *"Daniel's prophecy of the Son of Man 'coming in the clouds' was fulfilled in the Ascension of Christ."*

(Notice, they've got it backwards! They make Christ's ascension, his return!)

14. *"Ethnic Israel was excommunicated for its apostasy and will never again be God's Kingdom."*

(Friend, that is replacement theology, pure and simple.)

17. *"The Olivet Discourse is not about the Second Coming of Christ. It is a prophecy of the destruction of Jerusalem in A.D. 70." See they all go back to A.D. 70."*

18. *"The Great Tribulation took place in the fall of Israel. It will not be repeated and thus is not a future event."*

20. *"Although Israel will someday be restored to the true faith, the Bible does not tell of any future plan for Israel as a special nation."*

23. *"The 'Great Apostasy' happened in the first*

century. We therefore have no Biblical warrant to expect increasing apostasy as history progresses; instead, we should expect the increasing Christianization of the world."

24. *"The Last Days is a Biblical expression for the period between Christ's Advent and the destruction of Jerusalem in A.D. 70; the 'last days' of Israel."*

36. *"The 'Millennium' is the Kingdom of Jesus Christ, which He established at His First Advent."*

(Did you follow what he just wrote? The millennium began when Christ came two thousand years ago!)

38. *"The 'thousand years' of Revelation 20 is symbolic for a vast number of years, most likely many thousands."*

42. *"The center for the Christian reconstruction of the world is the Church."*[12]

(This is a Reconstructionist' teaching, plain and simple).

Many books are being written today, promoting "preterist beliefs" into the mainstream Christian world. Sadly, one of the most respected reformed theologians in the world today, Dr. R.C. Sproul, has apparently moved into the Preterist camp. In his book, entitled, "**The Last Days According to Jesus,**" with the sub-title, "*When Did Jesus Say He Would Return?*" Sproul writes,

"*Josephus's record of Jerusalem's fall indicates the radical fulfillment of Jesus' prophecy in the Olivet Discourse. As we have seen, preterists see in this event not only the destruction of the temple and its attending circumstances, but also the parousia of Christ his judgment-coming.*"13

Another author with a preterist viewpoint is Richard Abanes. In his book entitled "**End Time Visions – The Road to Armageddon,**" Richard Abanes likens all current prophecy preachers and authors to "P.T. Barnum."14

You remember what **P.T. Barnum** is famous for saying, don't you? *"There's a sucker born every minute."* According to this gentleman we lead our lives and our ministries under that premise. He said this, *"The observation is perfectly illustrated by the individuals obsessed with doomsday. They will believe practically anything as long as the person who is speaking has an air of authority."*15

Mr. Abanes goes on in this several hundred-paged book and names these individuals throughout this book in very critical terms and ways.

Who are these gentlemen, you ask?

Here is just a partial listing: *"Ray Brubaker, Dave*

*Breese, Charles Capps, J.R. Church, Paul and Jan
Crouch, John Hagee, Ed Hindson, Rex Humbard, Noah
Hutchings, Grant Jeffrey, Gary Kah, Tim LaHaye, Peter
and Paul LaLonde, David Allen Lewis, Hal Lindsey,
Chuck Missler, Rod Parsley, Pat Robertson, Lester
Sumrall, Charles Taylor, Jack Van Impe, John
Walvoord..."*[16]

In chapter eleven of Abanes' book, he passes
judgment upon all of these men by stating this. *"Prophecy
sells."* And then he asks the question, *"Are they
prophets... or profits?"*[17]

Let me show you why Mr. Abanes attacks the
futurists. In chapter ten of his book, Mr. Abanes explains
his personal interpretation of Matthew 24 and Jesus'
reference to the fig tree.

*"If Christian prophecy teachers were to be
consistent, then they would have to find numerous
countries to correspond to all the trees mentioned in
Luke."*[18]

Did you get the full understanding of that?

We Futurists believe the "fig tree" spoken of by
Jesus represents Israel. Abanes refutes this belief. He goes
on to say, *"It must be further recognized that nowhere in
Matthew 24 does Jesus declare that He is speaking to
some future generation."*[19]

Abanes is about to show his true "doctrinal colors."

He continues, *"One question, however, must be answered: If Jesus was telling the Jews present with him in the first century that they were the generation who would see 'the end,' then is he guilty of making a false prophecy? No. The 'end' about which he spoke may have been the end of Israel and Jerusalem in 70 A.D, not the end of the world. All of the 'signs' enumerated by Jesus took place in the first century just before the destruction of Jerusalem under the Roman Empire Titus. "*[20]

It appears that Mr. Abanes is a Preterist!

SEARCH THE SCRIPTURES

The validity of any particular view on end-time prophecy must be tested by the scriptures, NOT by the miscues of overzealous doomsayers that preceded us, no matter how long and consistently wrong their track record has been! There are biblical reasons that set this generation apart unlike any other that preceded us. This generation is unique.

There are Biblical reasons that set **THIS GENERATION** apart and unlike any other that preceded it---all pointing to the soon return of Christ!

This growing movement of scoffers is wanting you and I to begin to lay down our literal, fundamental, pre-millennial beliefs and convictions.

I was saddened, personally, when one of the finest

Christian magazines, **Charisma Magazine**, chose to do a cover story in mid-1999 about doomsday madness. Do you know who they chose to write the cover article? Richard Abanes! In his article entitled *"Why We Must Reject Millennium Madness,"* Richard Abanes said, *"...We will never know when, or even about when, the apocalypse will occur."*[21]

Abanes starts with a truth, but then very cunningly, links it to a non-truth. The first part of this statement is true, but the second part is not! Jesus clearly told us we cannot know the "exact time" of His coming. However, this was not ALL that Jesus told us. He went on to say, *"When you see all these things (begin to occur), KNOW that it is near, even at the doors." (Matthew 24:33)*

In other words, according to Jesus, we can know---in fact, we are commanded to know---something about the time and season, as we get **NEARER TO CHRIST'S RETURN!**

We're not supposed to be in the dark, sitting with our hands folded singing hymns, just hoping and praying, *"Well it might be next year. It might be a million years from now. You never really know, so why get caught up in that prophecy stuff anyhow. I'll just spend my money doing something else."*

We cannot know more than the Lord has revealed, but we ought not know less. According to Jesus, we are commanded to know something about the time and the seasons as we get nearer to the Coming of

Christ.

Be on your guard, against these *"Christian clergy preterists"* who can lead you from the truth. Stay in God's Word and listen to the Spirit speak to your heart.

Richard Abanes continues,

"Prophetic speculation continues to infect the Christian community. And with modern technology, the senseless ramblings of prophecy thumpers can now be spread faster and farther than ever before. Christians seem to care little that today's most prosperous end-time preachers have been repeatedly wrong."

"...no one has ever benefited from the disappointment and embarrassment inseparably linked to failed predictions about 'the end.' We will never know when, or even about when, the apocalypse will occur."[22]

To some, the above quote might even sound good. It almost sounds logical. It even almost sounds biblical. But is it?

Let's re-examine what Abanes has said. Abanes' reasoning is simply this: For two thousand years Alarmists have cried out, *"The time is at hand!"* And they've all been wrong. Right? Therefore his logic says, "All those who today say that the return of Christ is near, they, too, must be wrong."

Why does he say we're wrong? Because

everybody that preceded us for two thousand years was wrong. However, that is faulty logic. That is like somebody saying in 1945, *"You know, preachers have said for nineteen hundred and forty-five years that Israel would be reborn and they've all been wrong. So all these guys today are wrong."*

But guess what happened in 1948? Israel <u>was</u> reborn, thus setting this generation apart from all generations that preceded it.

In fact, the very nation of Israel itself is a real problem to the preterist scoffers. The preterists have no plausible explanation for this great miracle of history. The scoffers want us to believe that the re-establishing of the nation of Israel in our lifetime is merely a fluke, an accident of history. Yet today, for the first time since 586 BC, the Jewish people are living in their Biblical land under a sovereign government.

Never before in human history have a people been defeated, driven from their land, and dispersed among the many nations of the world, only to return over two millennia later and reclaim their country, language and identity. Never!

Yet Israel has accomplished this fact in our lifetime, and thus setting "this generation" apart, unlike any that has preceded it. How can any honest, Bible-believing Christian seriously entertain the possibility that this is not the hand of God at work? The scoffers in the land today would try and have us believe that all the prophetic declarations in the

Bible predicting this national rebirth of Israel in the last days, are somehow irrelevant and un-important.

Well I personally feel otherwise. Israel itself is Gods "super sign" that we are in fact living in the last days, and stands as a strong witness against the message of the modern scoffers of today.

Don't buy into any of those lies. No matter how they cloak it, no matter how they present it, no matter how they say it...don't receive what they have to say. The Preterists have their own agenda!

Yet another major Christian magazine, **CHRISTIANITY TODAY** also chose to address the subject of Bible Prophecy, namely the Book of Revelation. In the article, *"Revelation Now: Apocalypse Now"*, J. Nelson Kraybill writes,

"I largely take a Preterist view (emphasizing how Revelation may be describing circumstances of the first century). But the Word of God cannot be tethered to any one school of interpretation. In the end, I want parts of several methods of interpretation. I believe that much of Revelation describes the first century. The New Jerusalem is already breaking into our world....Parts of Revelation appear to be a handbook on present-day citizenship for the New Jerusalem."[23]

Once again, we discover the same trend. The Christian community is being force-fed the teaching of preterism!

There is bonafide evidence that this growing movement of scoffers wants you and I to begin to lay down our literal, fundamental, pre-millennial beliefs. But guess what? These "scoffing scholars" have some problems.

SEVEN DOCTRINAL PROBLEMS WITH THE SCOFFERS

They have some big problems with their premise. It starts to come out even in the words of their latest hero and their latest "star", Dr. R.C. Sproul.

He admits in the conclusion of his book,

"The purpose of The Last Days according to Jesus has been to examine and evaluate the various claims of preterism, both full and partial." In reference to the destruction of Jerusalem, Sproul states, *"This event certainly spelled the end of a crucial redemptive-historical epic. It must be viewed as the end of some age."*[24]

Even after hundreds of pages of writing, Dr. R.C. Sproul would not let himself get pinned down totally. The best he said was, *"Yeah, it's the close of some dispensation and age..."*

But Sproul seems unwilling to commit to the heretical view of full preterism because he says this, *"The great weakness of full preterism in what I regard to be its fatal flaw, is its treatment of the final resurrection. If full preterism is to gain wide credibility in our time it must overcome this obstacle."*[25]

Let's now examine seven doctrinal problems to the Preterist view.

PROBLEM NUMBER ONE.

Daniel's seventieth week. Daniel's seventieth week is Israel's hour to be delivered by God and turn to true faith in their Messiah. If you read it, that's what occurs. Jesus' description in the Olivet Discourse of the Tribulation period talks about divine deliverance and a rescue out of this terrible time of trouble.

Now why is that important?

When you examine the whole preterist position it is a contention and a theory of just the opposite.

There is a great book out called, "**THE GREAT TRIBULATION PAST OR FUTURE?**" co-authored by my friend Thomas Ice (a futurist) and Kenneth L. Gentry, Jr. (a preterist). These two evangelical theologians debate the question of "futurism" versus "preterism".

In this book, Thomas Ice asks the question:

"When were the Jews, who were under siege, rescued by the Lord in A.D. 70? They were not rescued; they were judged, as noted in Luke 21:20-24. But Matthew 24 refers to a divine rescue of those who are under siege (24:29-31). This could not have been fulfilled during the first century due to the fact that the Jewish Christian community fled Jerusalem before the final

siege. Matthew 24 refers to the deliverance of all Jews who are under siege. This did not happen under the first-century Roman siege. "26

Do you follow the logic? Jesus in the Olivet Discourse said that in the time of Tribulation, the time of Daniel's seventieth week, Israel would be rescued and restored by God. The Preterists would have us believe that the destruction of the temple in A.D. 70 which is supposedly the "fulfillment" of Daniel's seventieth week and the "fulfillment" of the tribulation period. They want us to believe that God "judged" Israel in 70 A.D. and thereby fulfilling all prophetic application of the coming "Tribulation."

No! This is completely opposite of what the prophets foretold. The judgment brought upon Jerusalem in 70 A.D. cannot be the fulfillment of Daniel's 70th week.

PROBLEM NUMBER TWO:

Christ's Coming. Jesus made some very clear statements within the Olivet Discourse concerning His physical literal coming. This is a major problem with Preterism, because the Preterists, in order to force a first-century fulfillment to Matthew 24, they've got to *"spiritualize"* all of His Comings. They've got to allegorize and create symbols out of all of Jesus' statements about His Return. Let me give you four examples.

Example Number One. Jesus said this, ***"Every eye will see Him at His Second Coming."*** Do you remember

He said that? How do they get around that fact? Again, from "**The Great Tribulation**", here's what Gentry writes,

"This is not a physical, visible coming, but a judgment-coming upon Jerusalem. They 'see' it in the sense that we 'see' how a math problem works: with the 'eye of our understanding' rather than the organ of vision."[27]

Did you see what he just did?

He took a literal declaration by Jesus that every physical eye would see Him; and totally spiritualized it. He went on to say, *"This actually refers to Jesus' ascension."* Oh my goodness. That's a good one. In other words when Jesus said, *"Every eye will see me at my Coming,"* he completely turns it upside down and makes the Second Coming the ascension.

He writes, *"This actually refers to Jesus ascension. In the destruction of the temple, the rejected Christ is vindicated as the ascended Lord and shown to possess great power and glory."*[28]

Do you see what they're saying? They reverse it. They've got it backwards! Why? It's because they are forced to make Christ's ascension also Christ's Return.

Example number two. Jesus mentions a sign in the heavens in the Olivet Discourse, revealing His Second Coming. How do they deal with this? Here's this quote from Kenneth Gentry,

"The 'sign' is not a visible token in the sky. Rather, the sign is that the 'Son of Man' rejected by the first-century Jews is in heaven. The destruction of Israel vindicates Christ. But what is 'the sign'? The temple's final destruction."[29]

They are forced to interpret "the sign" of Christ's return, as the actual destruction of the Jewish Temple. How absurd!

Example number three*.* Jesus mentioned "lightning" in the heavens at His Second Coming. How do they address this problem? Kenneth Gentry writes this,

"Matthew 24:27 says, 'For just as the lightning comes from the east, and flashes even to the west, so shall the coming of the Son of Man be.' Jesus warns His followers that He will not appear bodily in the first-century judgment. Nevertheless, He will 'come' in judgment like a destructive lightning bolt against Jerusalem. This coming, however, is a providential judgment coming, a Christ-directed judgment, rather than a miraculous, visible, bodily coming."[30]

You and I read where Jesus said He was going to physically return to earth and we believed Him. How dare you believe that? Oh, He came all right, only he came through the instrument of Titus and the Roman soldiers when they went in and destroyed Jerusalem and the temple. That's how Jesus came. That's what the preterists preach!! Do you believe it?

Example number four. Example four of why Christ's Coming is a problem for them is that *"Jesus said He would come in the clouds..."* Now how do they get around that? They're spiritualizing everything else. Are you ready for what he says? John Noe writes,

"So it happened. God removed that Jewish world (heaven and earth) in A.D. 70. All these prophecies and many others were fulfilled when the Roman armies, empowered by God, shook, removed, and left desolate the Temple, the city of Jerusalem and the whole world of biblical Judaism. This was the historical setting for Christ's coming on the clouds."[31]

In other words, they want you and I to believe that when the Temple was destroyed, and the clouds of smoke billowed up in the sky, that is what Jesus meant by Him coming in the clouds. Now, friend, if you believe that, you need a lot of prayer!

PROBLEM NUMBER THREE:

THE "DATE" ISSUE. The Preterists contend that all New Testament prophecies about the last days all occurred back at 70 A.D., including almost the entire book of Revelation! Nice theory, only one major problem....

If John wrote the Book of Revelation *AFTER* the Temple's destruction in 70 A.D., it would essentially destroy their entire premise. And every single Preterist teacher knows this fact.

The preterist defender, Kenneth L. Gentry, in his enthusiastic review of David Chilton's dominion theology book, "**DAYS OF VENGEANCE**", wrote, *"If it could be demonstrated that Revelation was written 25 years after the fall of Jerusalem, Chilton's entire labor would go up in smoke."*[32]

Does anyone know for sure *"when"* John the Revelator penned the Book of Revelation? The vast majority of scholars and church historians contend the time to be between 90-96 A.D.---some 25 years **AFTER** the destruction of Jerusalem!

Thomas Ice quotes Greek scholar and historian Kurt Aland in reference to the actual date when the Book of Revelation was written by the Apostle John.

"Aland says that revelation was 'written about the year 96'. If this is true, it renders the preterist's interpretation impossible, for Revelation is a prophecy about a future event."[33]

"The majority of scholars today think it unlikely that Revelation was written before A.D. 70. Instead, they favor the A.D. 95-96 date."[34]

There is a total absence of any historical references from the first three centuries following Christ to support the writing of Revelation prior to 70 A.D.

The preterist view is simply not true!

PROBLEM NUMBER FOUR:

CHURCH FATHERS. If the Preterists are right and Jesus returned to earth back in the first century as they contend, then surely we can find somebody, somewhere, back there in the first second and third century who believed and taught this fact. Right? We cannot find even one!

"If Preterists are right, not only did the whole world completely miss Christ's return on the clouds in glory, but so did virtually everyone in the church. Because with relatively few exceptions, practically every believer and 2,000 years of Christendom has believed Matthew 24:30 speaks of an event yet to happen."[35]

The historical record left by the church fathers refutes any validity to the preterist teachings.

PROBLEM NUMBER FIVE:

THE COMING RESURRECTION. Some preterists are partial preterists and some are full preterists. I believe "full" preterists are guilty of true heresy. True heresy is when you doctrinally deny one or more of the essentials of the faith. If you deny an essential, you preach heresy. We can differ on "non-essentials" all day; and still be brothers. But when you deny an essential you've got a problem. True heresy is when you deny the essentials. One of the *"essentials"* is the doctrine concerning the coming Resurrection.

Again quoting Dr. Ice, *"Such a position not only denies the hope of the Second Advent, but it also means that there will be no future resurrection of the saints. Such views are heretical." Dr. Gentry affirms, "Hyper-Preterism is heterodox. It is outside the creedal orthodoxy of Christianity." No creed allows any Second Advent in A.D. 70. No creed allows any other type of resurrection than a bodily one."*[36]

This is the major obstacle which Dr. Sproul expressed that I cited earlier. It's interesting to me because the Apostle Paul in the New Testament in 2 Timothy 2:15-18, addressed the hyper-Preterists of his day. He says,

"Study to shew thyself approved unto God, a workman that needeth not be ashamed, rightly dividing the word of truth. But shun profane and vain babblings: for they will increase unto more ungodliness. And their word will eat as doth a canker: of whom is Hy-me-nae'us and Phi-le'tus; who concerning the truth have erred..."

Now tell us, Paul, how have they erred? Keep reading. *"Saying that the resurrection is past already..."* In Paul's day there were some heretics who had erred from the truth, trying to get gullible, naïve Christians to believe that the resurrection already occurred. My friend, that is exactly and precisely what the scoffers are doing today. The extreme preterists believe that there is no future bodily resurrection, which places them **outside** the realm of Christian Orthodoxy.

Now you ask, *"Don't these men know this fact?"*

Oh yes. They not only know it; they revel in it. They know that their abhorrent interpretation puts them at odds with many of the Christian Orthodox creeds that we as Christians must uphold and adhere to.

Shockingly, they propose a change even within the essential doctrines of the church.

"So what shall we do with the creed? We recommend that their eschatological sections be revised-- lest we be enslaved to an incorrect and uninspired interpretation of Scripture. Our rule of faith and practice should be as follows: Jesus, in numerous places, clearly stated that His return would occur within the lifetime of His contemporaries. Every New Testament writer utilizes urgent and imminent language confirming the immediacy of His Return. We cannot overlook a biblical and time-restricted fulfillment in favor of man-made creeds and confessions,"[37]

For the hyper-preterists, even our historical doctrinal creeds can be "thrown aside" to accommodate their heretical agenda!

PROBLEM NUMBER SIX:

THE NEW HEAVEN AND THE NEW EARTH.
Most Preterists believe that we are currently living in at least an inaugurated new Heavens and new Earth.

Let's read 2 Peter 3: 10-13:

"But the day of the Lord will come as a thief in the night; in the which the heavens shall pass away with a great noise, and the elements shall melt with fervent heat, the earth also and the works that are therein shall be burned up. Seeing then that all these things shall be dissolved, what manner of persons ought ye to be in all holy conversation and godliness, Looking for and hasting unto the coming of the day of God, wherein the heavens being on fire shall be dissolved, and the elements shall melt with fervent heat? Nevertheless we, according to his promise, look for new heavens and a new earth, wherein dwelleth righteousness."

You thought you knew what that meant; but the Preterists are going to help us. John Noe says this about the new heavens,

"That means that our former earth consists of our unregenerated physical bodies, and our minds and our emotions. We can truly, fully, and individually become a new heaven and a new earth."

"The idea of a 'New Jerusalem' other than that which we already have in Christ is pure fantasy Christianity. The full descent of this Holy City, the New Jerusalem, 'coming down out of heaven from God' occurred immediately upon the demise of the old Jerusalem."[38]

My, are we foolish?

We didn't even know that the new heaven and the

new earth were here right now!!

Gary DeMar in an appendix within his book reprints David Chilton's bold declarations,

"The 'new heavens and earth' promised to the Church comprise the age of the New Covenant--the Gospel's triumph, when all mankind will come to bow down before the Lord. John Bray writes: 'This passage is a grand description of the gospel age after Christ came in judgment in 70 A.D. and took away the old heavens and the old earth. We now had the new heavens and the new earth of the gospel age. "[39]

Notice yet another quote from the preterist John Noe, *"Because Peter said the elements were going to melt with fervent heat... So what are these 'elements?' The 'elements' Peter is speaking of are the 'elementary principles' or 'rudiments' of Judaism, that Old Covenant 'world' or system, which would soon be destroyed in the coming of 'the day of the Lord' in A.D. 70. What was the fire? This divine 'fire' destroyed the Temple, the city, the sacrifices, the priesthood, the genealogies, the tribes, and the whole heart, soul and physical components of the Jewish religious system and theocracy--forever. Truly, Peter's 'world' that was soon to perish was the world of biblical Judaism; Old Covenant Israel. "*[40]

Once again, we find these scoffers taxing every latitude imaginable with the Word of God, and wrapping their preposterous conclusions around the clear prophetic statements of scripture.

PROBLEM NUMBER SEVEN:

OUR BLESSED HOPE. This entire theory and interpretation I believe robs the Church of our living, blessed hope. These false teachers are robbing our hope of Christ's Return from us. I believe that the New Testament teaching causes us to live in expectation of Christ's Return. When we live with that expectation, our focus shifts from the temporal and the earthly; to the eternal. We loosen our grip on the things of this world because we understand this world is not our home. We don't become distracted by worldly pursuits because they can't compare to the glory that awaits us.

A couple of years ago, I personally heard Gary DeMar, already quoted numerous times, a featured speaker at a workshop. His lecture revealed why he comes to the conclusion that he does. He explained that his current prophetic interest and teaching of preterism, as a result of his social and political agenda.

Make no mistake, friend, the preterists have a social agenda!

They grasped the theology of preterism to make their social agenda palatable to their minds. They have taught heretical views about the last days and preached them boldly, because they have a social, political agenda. They can't have one without the other.

You and I are the biggest threat they've got, because we still have a Blessed Hope!

We still have an expectation that Jesus is coming soon!

Mr. DeMar said, *"People, the reason we're in the mess we're in is because too many people have believed in doctrines like imminency. It's a theology of social irresponsibility and it will be devastating."*

In other words we are the biggest problem they've got because we preach that Christ's return to earth is imminent. We preach a Blessed Hope.

But what hope do the preterists offer you?

This is the hope that the preterists want to give us,

"If we figure the Biblical generation at about forty years, a thousand generations is forty-thousand years. Therefore we've got 36,600 years to go before this promise is fulfilled." <u>*And what promise is he talking about? ... The return of the Lord. Doesn't that just bless you?!*</u> *He went on to say this, "A figure of forty-thousand years is a bare minimum. This world has tens of thousands, perhaps hundreds of thousands of years of increasing godliness ahead of it before the Second Coming of Christ."*[41]

It's no wonder they don't want you to attend prophecy conferences. It's Christian Reconstructionism, plain and simple. They have to preach this messed-up eschatology, because it's the only way to justify their political agenda. They are anticipating tens and hundreds of thousands of years of Christian advancement, before Jesus will physically return to earth! These scoffers are trying to rob the church of her blessed hope!

If you honestly read the New Testament and you read the verses and the passages concerning Christ's Coming, you will discover that when we live our lives expecting Christ's imminent Return, it motivates us to a greater level of holiness and obedience to God.

When we understand that at any moment now we will be caught up to face our Lord and give an account for our lives---we become more eager to do His will on earth.

John said it well in I John 3:3, **"For every man hath in them this hope..."**

What hope?

THE BLESSED HOPE.

"He purifies himself even as He is pure." Whoever highlights the coming of Christ is also responsible to teach the importance of a pure life.

Chuck Swindoll says, **"What is a true sign of heresy? It is a ministry that emphasizes the Lord's Return but does not with equal gusto emphasize a Godly life."**

This is a prophetic hour. The season of prophetic fulfillment of all that God has spoken for these last days.

We who believe in a pre-Tribulation Rapture of the Church, must stop trying to calculate the exact day of Christ's Return, or the Rapture of the Church. These foolish speculations are merely giving more fuel to our scoffers and critics.

We must preach a TRUE prophetic word in this hour!

What is a true prophetic minister going to look like and talk like during these last days?

I believe the true prophecy preachers of this last day are going to be like John the Baptist, and boldly proclaim, *"Repent and flee the wrath to come!"*

John Bevere, in his book, **"THUS SAITH THE LORD"** says it best, *"Very little of what is happening in our prophetic conferences and our meetings and our services today even remotely correlates with Jesus or John the Baptist pattern of prophecy."*

"The prophetic ministry God is raising up in these latter days will be after the order of John the Baptist. Their ministries will trumpet the same call and warning as his. These prophets will call for change. Their primary mission will be turning the hearts of God's people back to their Father. Their messages will be accompanied by strong conviction. Often the words might seem nice. Their preaching will hit the hardest areas of our hearts as a hammer smashing upon a rock. They will command and rebuke and correct and exhort with all

authority, yet it all will flow from a heart filled with love for God and His people. These prophets will not seek the accolades or rewards of man. They will only desire to handle faithfully the truth that sets men free. They will not be bought, for they already know their rewarder. Power, popularity or money will not influence their words. They are the Elijah prophets who will speak as the oracles of God, alight with Holy Fire and their words will act as skillfully-guided missiles targeting the hearts of men. "[42]

No matter what the scoffers may say, are you ready for His imminent return?

Are you pursuing a holy lifestyle?

Are you obedient to God and His Word?

May God grant to you His Blessed Hope!

Jesus is coming soon! **Be Ready!**

FOOTNOTES

1. John Noe, *Beyond the End Times*, back cover.
2. Ibid.
3. Ibid., p. 69.
4. Ibid., p. 268.
5. Ibid., p. 269.
6. Gary DeMar, *Last Days Madness*, p. 33.
7. Ibid., p. 47.
8. John Noe, *What is the Preterist View?*
9. John F. MacArthur, *The Second Coming*, p. 11.
10. John Noe, *Beyond the End Times*, p. 98.
11. Gary DeMar, *Last Days Madness*, p. 48.
12. David Chilton, *Paradise Restored*, p. 223-225.
13. R.C. Sproul, *The Last Days According to Jesus*, p. 127.
14. Richard Abanes, *End-Time Visions – The Road to Armageddon?*, *p. 317.*
15. Ibid.
16. Ibid. (throughout).
17. Ibid., p. 308.
18. Ibid., p. 298.
19. Ibid.
20. Ibid.
21. Richard Abanes, "Why We Must Reject Millennium Madness," *CHARISMA*, July, 1999, p.40.
22. Ibid.
23. J. Nelson Kraybill, "APOCALYPSE NOW," *CHRISTIANITY TODAY*, October 24, 1999.
24. R.C. Sproul, *The Last Days According to Jesus*, p. 202.

25. Ibid., P. 203.
26. Thomas Ice and Kenneth L. Gentry, Jr., *The Great Tribulation Past or Future?*, p. 125.
27. Ibid., p. 60.
28. Ibid., p. 61.
29. Ibid., p. 59.
30. Ibid., p. 53.
31. John Noe, *Beyond the End Times*, p. 239.
32. Kenneth L. Gentry, Jr., *The Council Chalchedon*, Vol. 11, No. 4, p.11.
33. Thomas Ice and Kenneth L. Gentry, Jr., *The Great Tribulation Past or Future?*, p. 111.
34. Ibid., p. 112.
35. John F. MacArthur, *The Second Coming*, p. 123.
36. Thomas Ice and Kenneth L. Gentry, Jr., *The Great Tribulation Past or Future?*, p. 162.
37. John Noe, *Beyond the End Times*, p. 216.
38. Ibid., p. 255, 261.
39. Gary DeMar, *Last Days Madness*, p. 496.
40. John Noe, *Beyond the End Times*, p. 246.
41. David Chilton, *Paradise Restored*, p. 221.
42. John Bevere, *Thus Saith the Lord?*, p. 38, 34.

APPENDIX

The following italics and bold face quotes are taken directly from an early 2000 official mailing from Edward E. Stevens, president of the International Preterists Association, Inc. It definitely shows they are seeking large funding for their political and social agendas.

"The International Preterist Association (IPA) is poised to launch a major national advertising and publicity campaign to take on, head-to-head, the 'Left Behind' series and introduce the Preterist view of Bible prophecy to millions of new people this year.

This is very exciting – a historic first!

'Left Behind' Series Prompts Campaign

The wildly popular "Left Behind" series of futurist-rapture books by Tim LaHaye and Jerry Jenkins is capturing massive attention. But we believe it is tragically deluding millions in the process. Virtually no one is voicing concern or offering a biblical alternative. That must change!

I believe God expects us preterists to challenge LaHaye's and Jenkins' flawed theology, and present – in a dynamic way – what the Bible really says about the time of Jesus' return."

The Preterists have a three-step plan:

"First Campaign Objective: Place a series of paid ads...in major Christian magazines such as World and Christianity Today.

Second Campaign Objective: Launch a major publicity campaign aimed at Christian leaders via direct mail, convention booths, and Christian conferences.

Third Campaign Objective: Present Preterism on Christian and secular radio and television programs, and in newspaper articles and reviews."

This next portion shows why they need much finances to accomplish their agendas:

"Why We Need Your Help

Even a modest David versus Goliath (i.e. preterists versus the "Left Behind" big guys) campaign like the one I have just outlined could easily cost $500,000 or more to do it right.

Expensive? Yes! A major challenge for a movement our size? Yes! But I believe God will provide through you just what He wants us to use, and we will go only as far and as fast as He enables us to through your generosity.

People can not consider the Preterist view if they don't know it exists. Our ads in magazines and other media will introduce them. Positioning ourselves against the "Left Behind" series will be a real media draw. The controversial "buzz" about this could propel Preterism into the spotlight and generate some significant spin-off radio and television coverage.

God has uniquely positioned us to seize this opportunity. He has provided the tools, the strategy, and the message. The timing is right. And we are doing it only for His glory.

"My heart's desire and prayer to God" is to introduce Preterism to the movers and shakers of conservative Christianity, to capture major media attention, and get millions of new people thinking about the AD 70 fulfillment of Bible prophecy!"

I, too, wake up with the same burning passion in my heart to stop you from robbing the Church of OUR BLESSED HOPE!

He reveals his arrogance by stating,

"I'm convinced that once the full implications of the Preterist view begin to dawn on folks, the Reformation will explode and eventually dwarf the impact of the first Reformation. Yes, you heard me right. We are living in the most pivotal generation since the first century."

He honestly believes his heretical position needs to create another Reformation and bring much change that will dwarf the impact of the Reformation!

There are other groups, even now, that are planning

to distribute tens of thousands of anti-Rapture pamphlets in theatres where the "Left Behind" movie will be showing. Truly, they are literally trying to ride on the coat-tails of the "Left Behind" phenomenon.

I commend Dr. Tim LaHaye and Dr. Jerry Jenkins. God has clearly put His hand of blessing on the "Left Behind" series. Obviously, there are those in the Preterist's camp who choke when they try to swallow the success of the "Left Behind" movie and book.

Who do they think they are to plan to shatter the theology and success of "Left Behind"? Not only is their theology off, but their spirit is not a spirit to be desirous of; and God simply will not bless the preterist's efforts.

This letter (with direct quotes in bold italics) was printed and sent out by the International Preterist Association, Inc. in Bradford, Pennsylvania. The response card for this particular mailing reads:

"Let's Reach Millions with the Preterist Message!

Yes, Ed! I will help International Preterist Association launch this nationwide campaign to introduce Preterism to millions of new people---the first step in igniting the next Reformation."

This is their agenda. These people have a specific agenda; and this is the proof.

--Dr. Joe Van Koevering

NOTES

SUBSCRIBE TO ONE
OF THE FOREMOST PROPHECY
MAGAZINES IN THE WORLD!

GOD'S NEWS BEHIND THE NEWS

Keen prophetic insights into the future have riveted so many readers. This beautiful magazine will not only be an inspiration to you, but a source of genuine encouragement.

This relevant, color magazine highlights world news events that actually fulfill Bible prophecies today. Issue after issue, you can more fully understand what is actually happening in our world; and how it relates to YOU!

The most outstanding prophetic scholars in the world have been highlighted to give the most up-to-date information possible. I've heard from many friends who say that their life has literally been changed because of the magazine.

The subscription rate for a year is $22.50 ($37.50 for TWO years!). At God's News, we want to minister to you and your family right there in the comfort of your home.

Call 1-800-366-1463

THE AUTHOR

DR. JOE VanKOEVERING . . .

His worldwide, anointed teaching and preaching ministry has taken him to numerous states and other countries. He is the co-host of the world-known International Prophecy Conference.

Dr. Van Koevering's dynamic personality and smiling face is recognized by millions around the world through Joe's co-hosting of the weekly, internationally-syndicated television program, GOD'S NEWS BEHIND THE NEWS. He was elected by the Board of God's News Behind the News to be its CEO. He has shared the program with the greatest prophecy scholars alive today, helping him to fulfill the original call upon his life.

Rev. Van Koevering has the heart of a pastor. He currently pastors Gateway Christian Center, St. Petersburg, Florida, where he exercises his passion for teaching the Word of God.

For further information, contact:
Dr. Joe VanKoevering
God's News Behind the News
P.O. Box 10475
St. Petersburg, FL 33733